Machine Embroidered Woodlands

Dedication
To my mum

Machine Embroidered
Woodlands

Alison Holt

SEARCH PRESS

First published in Great Britain 2009

Search Press Limited
Wellwood, North Farm Road,
Tunbridge Wells, Kent TN2 3DR

Text copyright © Alison Holt 2009

Photographs by Debbie Patterson, Search Press Studios;
Roddy Paine Photographic Studio; and Myk Briggs,
myk@thebakery

Photographs and design copyright © Search Press Ltd. 2009

ISBN: 978-1-84448-273-3

Suppliers
If you have difficulty in obtaining any of the materials and
equipment mentioned in this book, please visit our website
at www.searchpress.com.

Publishers' note
All the step-by-step photographs in this book feature the
author, Alison Holt, demonstrating machine embroidery.
No models have been used.

Acknowledgements

*Many people have contributed to the content of
this book, and this is where they get
a well-deserved mention. I would like to give
them all my heart-felt thanks.*

*To Katie, my editor, for all her enthusiasm and hard
work; to Myk Briggs, Debbie Patterson and
Gavin Sawyer for their expert photography; to Aurifil
for generously supplying me with their lovely threads
(www.aurifil.it); to my family for their continued
support and encouragement; and to my students for
their eager anticipation of this book, which gave me
the incentive to write it!*

Front cover
Spring Woodland
*Silver birch trees, azaleas and ferns combine to
create a range of textures in this springtime scene.*

Page 1
The Mossy Stream
18 x 25.5cm (7 x 10in)

*The texture of the moss is captured here by using
tiny, closely worked stitches.*

Page 2
Snow Carpet
10 x 14cm (4 x 5½in)

*A limited palette of green, white and brown
provides a striking composition.*

Page 3
Dappled Shadows
18 x 13cm (7 x 5in)

*The pattern of shadows on the tree is the focal
point of this embroidery.*

Contents

Snow Shadows
10 x 23cm (4 x 9in)
*The strong blue shadows across the snow create
perspective and depth in this winter woodland scene.*

Introduction

I love my regular walks through local woodlands; there is so much to be inspired by, and the changing seasons feed my passion for interpreting nature in machine embroidery all year round. As winter snowdrops fade away, they are soon replaced by primroses and daffodils. There is freshness and vitality to this time of year, with bright green ferns unfurling and fresh new buds everywhere. For me, yellow is the colour of spring; even the new shoots on the trees are a lime or yellow-green. I eagerly look for other signs of spring such as blossom, bluebells and wild garlic, adding more colours to the landscape. As the seasons progress, azaleas and rhododendrons, which my garden has in abundance, change the palette to reds, purples, pinks and orange.

The summer brings trees in full leaf, creating dappled shadows on the dry, dusty pathways of last autumn's fallen leaves. Strong tones, dark shadows and bright sunlight provide dramatic contrasts, and the richly coloured, mossy trees, woodland streams, ferns and dense foliage provide a vast range of greens that are a great source of inspiration to me.

The Mossy Wall
13 x 18cm (5 x 7in)
Spring foliage on the trees and autumn leaves on the ground supply the rich colour scheme of this embroidery.

Daffodils at Chirk Castle
10 x 15cm (4 x 6in)
These drifts of daffodils are worked using a zigzig stitch, increasing in size towards the foreground to achieve perspective. This technique is shown on page 33.

When autumn arrives the leaves start to change colour; green turns to yellow then rust, red and orange. This is a very exciting time in terms of colour, texture and detail. Swathes of bracken slowly change to subtle shades of brown, contrasting with the grassy paths and silver birch trees. There is a feeling of richness and warmth in the colour palette that belies the onset of winter.

As winter leaf-fall reveals the bare branches of the trees, you become aware of the patterns formed by the branches, and the angles and shapes between them. When highlighted by frost and snow, coupled with a blue sky and winter sunlight, an inspiring scene is created. When snow falls I brave the cold as quickly as possible to try to get the perfect photograph. I look for foreground interest, texture, contrast, strong silhouettes and features that draw my eye into the distance, creating depth and perspective. There is a limited palette at this time of year, but copper beech and oak trees, bracken and fallen leaves provide some colour, as do strong, blue shadows stretching across fallen snow – my favourite subject for a winter scene!

In this book, I guide you carefully through all the elements for creating a woodland in stitch, starting with the basics of materials, picture composition, choosing thread colours and starting to stitch and ending with four projects, each depicting woodlands at different times of the year. I hope, through using this book, you are as inspired as I am by the ever-changing seasons and their effect on the countryside, and will venture out with your camera to capture awe-inspiring scenes of your own to transform into machine embroideries.

Materials and equipment

After many years of working with machine embroidery and silk painting, I have learnt a lot about the materials and equipment available, and have developed some personal favourites. In this chapter, I hope to pass on to you some valuable information to help you choose which products to buy when first setting out in this area of embroidery.

Threads

There is a wide variety of threads suitable for machine embroidery – as long as they are good quality and colourfast, which you use is down to personal preference. My favourite is a fine (no. 50), pure cotton thread; I like the fine weight and subtle sheen of the natural fibres. I always buy threads in tonal ranges as these are more useful for the way I like to blend colours in my work. To increase the range of colours available to me, I buy several different makes and weights of machine thread.

I own numerous threads, in a broad range of colours and tones, which means I can almost always find the exact colour I am looking for when working on an embroidery. I store all my threads in colour-coded trays and find this makes selecting colours easier.

Sewing machine

You can use any electric sewing machine to do machine embroidery, but it is important that the machine is well-maintained and oiled regularly for trouble-free sewing. It is possible to adapt a basic electric sewing machine very easily for creative machine embroidery. You need to be able to remove the presser foot and lower the feed dog, which will allow you to move the embroidery in various directions and at any speed. If the machine is set into a table, this is ideal, but otherwise a table attachment is necessary to support the embroidery hoop, which allows you to slide your work smoothly under the needle for better control. A machine that has a swing needle and therefore does zigzag stitch as well as straight stitch will give you more variety of texture, and I prefer a dial or sliding lever to alter the stitch width because it gives more flexibility than push-button controls.

My sewing machine, with its table attachment and the presser foot removed.

Silk

I have tried many different types and weights of fabric for painting and embroidery, and my favourite is a medium-weight, 8mm habutai silk. It paints beautifully, and you can stretch it really taut in the frame. It works well with the number and scale of the stitches my work entails, and it has an even weave and natural sheen which complement the cotton threads I use.

Embroidery hoop

You will need a 20cm (8in) wooden embroidery hoop with the inner hoop bound with fabric tape. A bound hoop helps grip the silk more effectively, which keeps the fabric flat and taut during stitching and prevents puckering.

Machine bobbins

A selection of spare bobbins is useful, each wound with a different-coloured thread, because of the many colour changes needed during machine embroidery.

The basic materials and items of equipment you will need for machine embroidery.

Screwdrivers

A small screwdriver is needed to alter the tension screw on the bobbin, and a larger one to tighten the screw on the hoop.

Machine needles

I always use a size 80 (12) needle. Make sure it is in good condition because a blunt needle will make pull lines in the silk.

Embroidery scissors

A sharp pair of embroidery scissors is essential for cutting threads close to the surface of your work.

9

Equipment for transferring the design

Source photographs

Photographs are essential; they are the inspiration for, and the starting point of, every embroidery.

L-shaped cards

These help you decide on the final size and composition of your design by allowing you to crop your photographs in different ways.

Air / water-soluble pen

This is used to draw out the basic design and details on the silk. It is air/water-soluble, which means it will fade gradually with time but can also be removed with water.

Resist

Resist is a clear gel that I use to mark the outlines of the basic elements of my design on the silk. It comes in a plastic pipette with a fine (0.3mm) nib, and when dry it stops the flow of the silk paints, preventing the background colours from spreading into each other. When the dyes have been fixed, the resist can be washed out with hot, soapy water leaving white lines in its place.

Masking tape

I use masking tape to attach my source photograph to the back of the silk so that I can trace the basic design on to the silk with the air/water-soluble pen. I also use it to hold the L-shaped cards in place when cropping the photographs.

Ruler

I always draw a frame around my designs to make sure the edges of the picture are straight and square, and for this I use a metal ruler. If you use the ruler to draw a line with resist, be careful not to smudge the wet line when moving the ruler away.

Silk painting equipment

Silk frame

I use a simple, square wooden frame to stretch the silk on for painting. This keeps the fabric flat and square, and raised above the table to allow the paint to spread evenly across the surface.

Silk pins

These are three-pronged metal pins used to secure the silk on to the frame.

Water pot

You will need a container of water in which to clean your brushes and to dilute the silk paints, making them paler in tone.

Silk paints

Silk paints are water based and can be used straight from the bottle to give the strongest tone, or watered down to make them paler. They can also be mixed together to make new colours. They are fixed to the silk by ironing with a hot iron once they are dry.

Palette

I prefer to use a white ceramic palette in which to mix my paints because it allows you to see clearly the colours you are mixing; it is easy to wash clean; and it does not discolour like plastic.

Paintbrushes

I use watercolour paintbrushes in a range of sizes from 000 up to 8. The larger brushes are for washes of colour and the smaller sizes for the fine details.

Paper towel

This is useful for removing excess paint from the brush when trying to achieve a fine line, and also for drying my brush after washing it to prevent the paints I have mixed being watered down.

Inspiration

Nature is a constant inspiration to me; whether I am out walking the dog or driving in the car, there is always something new to see: an unexpected snowfall, or an early morning sunrise with the most amazing sky contrasting with the dark silhouettes of winter trees.

The quality of light changes not only throughout the day but also with the changing seasons, producing an endless source of ideas for my work. I have my camera with me all the time, and I use photographs as a starting point for all my embroideries.

Using photographs

Photography is a great way of capturing and storing pictures that can be used as a basis for your embroideries, particularly if you cannot draw. I use photographs as a starting point for my own design ideas, as well as detail and colour references.

I try to compose my photographs carefully, interpreting the scene as a potential embroidery before taking the shot, but photographs can be cropped or joined together to improve the composition, or reduced in size to make them more manageable (I often make my embroideries the same size as the source photograph). Elements can be left out or moved within a picture, or parts of different photographs combined. Try taking the foreground of one photograph and putting it with the background of another; this can work very well. In woodland scenes, I often thin out the number of branches to open out a scene and make it less complicated.

New Shoots and Bells
11.5 x 13cm (4½ x 5in)

The source photograph shown above, right has been cropped to form a portrait rather than a landscape picture. I intentionally made a gap between the foreground tree and those behind it. This opens up the picture, clarifies the position of the trees and creates perspective. More bluebells were added to the foreground using other photographs for reference.

Autumn Bank

13 x 28cm (5 x 11in)

The two source photographs, shown above, were joined together to produce the final composition. The hand-painted rocks combined with the stitched moss, foliage and tree trunks produce an interesting mixture of textures and techniques.

Composition

Composition is essentially the arrangement of elements within a picture. There should be a focal point, which can be a foreground tree or a swathe of woodland flowers, and when positioning this within the frame, balance and proportion are taken into account. We have a natural tendency to divide a picture into one-third and two-thirds, and to place strong elements at points that divide it either vertically or horizontally.

A strong design can be created using series of lines. Curved lines formed by pathways or branches suggest movement and depth; straight vertical and horizontal lines formed by trees or shadows give a picture structure and strength; diagonal lines are used to lead the eye in.

Contrast is an essential ingredient in a good composition. It can be achieved using complementary colours, such as red and green, or different textures, such as smooth tree trunks and textured fallen leaves. I use painted areas, which are smooth, alongside stitched areas, which are rough. A broad tonal range, with dark shadows and bright spots of sunlight, also provides contrast; a variety of shapes, such as straight tree trunks in rows mixed with randomly placed foliage, also enhances the composition. Just enough contrast will create interest; too much will result in chaos and confusion.

Repeating elements in a picture is a good design strategy, giving rhythm and unity to the composition. In a woodland scene, this could be achieved by row upon row of bluebells or a line of trees.

A

B

First Frost

28 x 13cm (11 x 5in)

I loved the composition of photograph A, with the path leading the eye into the distance, the gentle curve of frosty grass cutting through the bracken and the stark winter trees, but I felt the right-hand side of the photograph was weak and needed a well-defined element to strengthen it. I 'borrowed' a tree from photograph B and made a strong, well-balanced composition with all the elements I wanted.

Snow

7.5 x 7.5cm (3 x 3in)

The focal point of the source photograph was cropped out to form a small but strong composition.

A Sudden Fall of Snow

23 x 15cm (9 x 6in)

For this embroidery, the source photograph on the right was cropped at the top, then enlarged, and the distant trees were thinned out to reveal more of the sky. This created depth. The strong contrast of dark winter trees and quickly melting snow gives the picture a sense of drama.

Colour

It is often the colours that attract me to a scene – I seek out bright, colourful autumn foliage with its complementary colours of reds and greens, and I love the strong contrast of white, blue, black and dark brown found on a frosty winter's day. These elements produce a sense of drama that will translate well into an embroidered picture.

Having an understanding of colour, and how different colours are linked and composed, can help you identify the colours in your photograph, and to translate them accurately into the threads and silk paints you need to complete your embroidery. For example, being able to distinguish a blue-green from a yellow-green will allow you to introduce subtle variations in colour, which in turn will result in a more realistic interpretation of nature.

Be aware that colours change, too, from distance to foreground. The muted greens, soft blues and grey-greens in the distance become brighter, stronger and more vibrant and with a wider tonal range in the foreground; this is where you find the lightest and darkest colours side by side.

Autumn Walk
16.5 x 25.5cm (6½ x 10in)
Rich autumn colours – reds, yellows and greens – give this scene huge visual impact.

16

Interpreting colour in thread

Before I start to stitch, I gather together all the threads I need for the embroidery. To obtain the best match I can with the colours in the source photograph, I always do this in good, natural light. I start by choosing one colour within an area, such as a tree or a shrub, and then add lighter and darker shades of that colour until I have the full tonal range needed to replicate that particular element. I then move from area to area, repeating the process until I have selected all the colours needed for the whole picture. At the same time, I may make notes of what goes where, and this is particularly helpful if you are a beginner.

Reassess your choices at regular intervals during the embroidery stage, and be prepared to vary your selection – I often add an extra colour or two as my work progresses.

Achieving subtle variations in colour

If the perfect match in thread cannot be found, I mix or blend two colours together by putting one thread in the bobbin and one on the top of the machine, to achieve just the right shade. For example, if the nearest match I can find to a green within some foliage is not quite yellow enough, I put it on the top of the machine with a yellow thread in the bobbin, and pull the yellow to the surface by increasing the top tension. The eye mixes the two together and the green appears more yellow. Similarly, if a blue thread is the right colour but not pale enough, an off-white thread pulled up from the bobbin will blend with it and make it appear paler in tone.

This blending of colours by the eye is similar to pointillism in art, in which small, distinct spots of colour are used to create the impression of a much wider colour range. This effect will give your embroideries a depth and vibrancy that those using single, flat tones will lack.

To achieve blending and shading in my work, I change one colour at a time on the machine. A different-coloured bobbin thread can subtly affect the overall appearance of the top thread, as shown by the samples below. Each sample is worked in parallel lines of straight stitch, and I have used the same green thread on top for each of the samples. In the first sample on the left I have used the same colour in the bobbin as on the top, then, moving across to the right, changed it to dark green, pale yellow, white and mid yellow.

I find holding the reels of thread over the photograph works well, rather than just using a single thread.

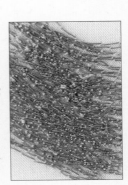

Starting to stitch

There are a few essential steps to follow before you can use your machine for freehand machine embroidery.

Adapting the machine

The first thing you need to do is to remove the presser foot and lower the feed dog; consult the instruction manual for your machine if you are unsure how to do this. This will allow you to move the embroidery in any direction and at any speed, giving you control of the length and direction of the stitches. If you move the hoop slowly you will get small stitches; if you move it quickly you will get longer stitches.

Stitch tension

Altering the thread tension on the sewing machine will have different effects that you can use for creating texture and blending colours. To pull the bobbin thread up into loops so that it is visible on the surface of the embroidery, loosen the bobbin thread or tighten the tension on the top thread.

    The bobbin is loosened by turning the small screw on the bobbin case anti-clockwise. If you are nervous about doing this, buy a spare bobbin case specifically for freehand machine embroidery and keep it permanently adjusted. The top tension is tightened by moving the tension dial to a higher number or towards the plus sign; loosen the top tension by moving the dial in the opposite direction.

Stretching the fabric in a hoop

Before you start to embroider, bind the inner hoop with fabric tape in order to obtain a better grip on the fabric, and stretch the fabric really tight in the hoop. This is important to prevent the fabric from puckering and to obtain a neater finish to your work. If the machine appears to miss stitches, or breaks a thread or a needle, this may be because the fabric is not taut enough in the hoop.

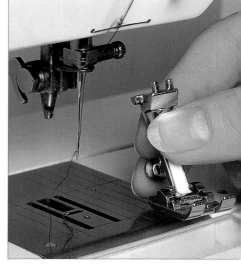

Removing the presser foot. Note that the feed dog has been lowered so that it is no longer visible.

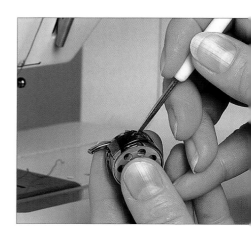

Turning the tension screw on the bobbin case.

Push the inner hoop down into the outer hoop. As you stretch the fabric, make sure the painted background is square in the hoop, with straight edges. Tighten the screw to keep the fabric taut.

Starting to sew

Alway start with the most distant part of the composition. Place the hoop and fabric under the machine, with the hoop 'upside down' so that the fabric lies flat on the bed of the machine. Lower the presser bar to engage the top tension and pull up the bobbin thread, holding it with the top thread to prevent them tangling. Both threads can be cut off after you have worked a few stitches.

All of my embroideries are made using straight stitch and zigzag stitch; all I vary is the stitch length (by altering the speed at which I move the hoop) and the width of the zigzag (by changing the width setting on the machine). The various textures and other effects I create result from the way in which I move the hoop and alter the thread tension. To help you get started, some of these effects are explained on the following three pages. If you are new to freehand machine embroidery, practise these techniques to improve your coordination and control and to get a feel for what can be achieved.

Tip

Experiment by keeping the machine speed constant and vary the speed at which you move the hoop; also with different bobbin and top tensions. This will give you an idea of the various effects you can achieve before you start an embroidery.

The correct way to hold the hoop under the machine. To have the best control, rest your forearm or elbow on the table and make sure the movements you make are with your fingers and not your arms.

Basic stitches

My approach to machine embroidery is to think like a painter, and use the sewing machine as a paintbrush. This is how I turn my source photograph into an embroidery: I think in stitch. The sewing machine can only give me a fine line with straight stitch or a broad line when set on zigzag, and I use these stitches in a variety of sizes, directions and colours to achieve different effects.

Straight stitch

Use straight stitch to draw fine lines using either small or large stitches; and for fine texture, it makes a wonderful filler stitch. Experiment with various speeds and types of movement of the hoop to obtain different effects.

This sample has a red thread on the top of the machine and a yellow bobbin thread pulled to the surface by a tight top tension.

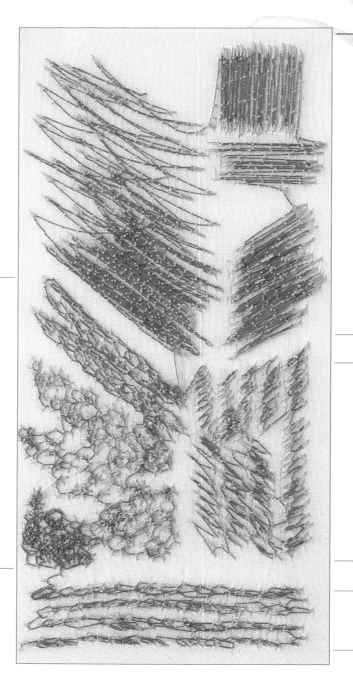

Parallel rows of straight stitch worked horizontally, vertically or diagonally, in straight lines and in curves.

Spiralling hand movements create a fine overall texture. The spirals can be round or lozenge-shaped, and worked in curves, horizontally or diagonally to fill in any shape.

A small, jagged hand movement gives small, jagged stitches that can be worked in any shape or direction.

Horizontal, spiralling hand movements.

Zigzag stitch

This gives a bolder, broader line to draw with than straight stitch, and is very versatile. It can be smooth or textured, worked in broken marks or in a continuous line, and placed lying in different directions by rotating the angle of the hoop. Remember to experiment with altered tensions and various widths of zigzag.

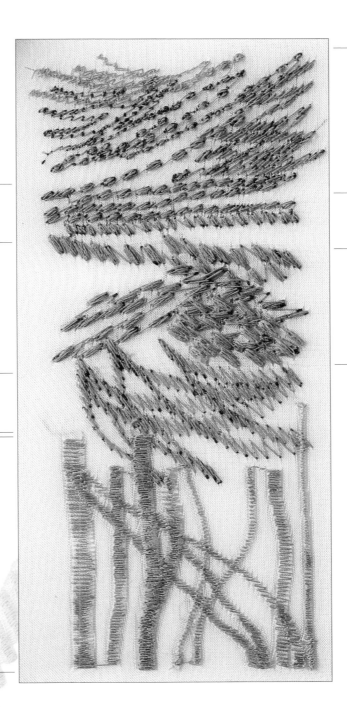

Use a wider zigzag and work the stitches on the spot by holding the hoop still for the stitches to build up on top of each other. Move the hoop a short distance and repeat.

A narrow width of zigzag and the hoop moved slowly along a curved line.

The widest zigzag stitch is used here. Place the stitches in various directions and overlapping each other.

Moving the hoop at a constant speed in a diagonal curve.

Moving the hoop at a slow and consistent speed in a vertical direction gives a column of zigzag; these can be various widths, straight or curved.

21

Zigzag stitch, varying width

To change the stitch width as you sew, use one hand to move your embroidery under the needle, and the other to gradually turn the dial on the machine (this technique is harder to master on a machine with push-button controls). If spaces appear between the stitches, move the hoop more slowly; if the stitching becomes too textured, move it faster. Using a darker bobbin thread and bringing it to the surface by tightening the top tension creates a more three-dimensional effect.

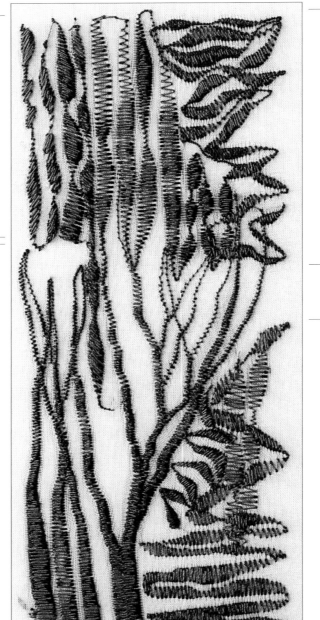

Move the hoop at an angle to make the zigzag stitches tilt within the shape.

Work columns that decrease in width as you approach the top. You can form several branches using this method.

Vary the speed of the hoop to alter the spacing of the stitches, and vary the stitch width to form shapes. Rotate the hoop 90° to lay the stitches horizontally.

Zigzags of varying width worked in curved shapes, both horizontally and vertically, and overlapping each other.

Planning your embroidery

Before you start an embroidered woodland scene, look at and analyse the overall shapes of the different elements in the picture, for example is the foliage rounded, vertical, diagonal, jagged, small or large? Think about the sorts of marks you would make with a pencil if you were drawing the picture; which directions they would lie in and what size they would be. How would you move the pencil to recreate what you can see in the photograph? The next step is to translate these marks into stitches – straight stitches and zigzag stitches – and the way you move the hoop. To make this process easier, draw a sketch of the design. This is the stage at which you can move or remove elements of your chosen composition if you feel it would improve it, for example increasing the amount of sky and light in a woodland scene helps open it out and create more depth.

An example of one of my sketches is shown here, together with the source photograph and the finished embroidery, which I hope will give you an insight in to the kinds of thought processes you will need to go through yourself when planning a piece of work.

The completed embroidery. Strong, dark tree trunks formed with vertical, parallel rows of straight stitch contrast well with the horizontal zigzag stitches used for the autumn foliage.

23

Creating a woodland in stitch

A woodland can be divided into various elements – the trees, foliage, woodland floor, woodland flowers, etc. – and experience has taught me the best ways of creating these elements, and of achieving perspective, light and shade, and so on. In this section of the book I hope to provide you with a directory of tried-and-tested techniques for all the elements found within a woodland scene, all of which are used in the projects on pages 42–79.

Light and shade

This is an important part of woodland scenes and, when used effectively, can create a wonderful sense of atmosphere and drama. The deep shadows cast by trees and their foliage, especially in winter and summer, give a strong pattern and rhythm to a design, as can the stripes falling across the woodland floor created by the sunlight streaming through the trees. Be aware of the direction of light falling on to tree trunks and foliage, be bold in your choice of colours, and use a tonal range that extends from very dark to very light. To create shadows in a bluebell wood or on snow, for example, you will need the darkest shades in your thread box; at the other end of the range, you will need white and off-white to create highlights on leaves or snow in sunlight.

Snowdrop Walk
13 x 18cm (5 x 7in)

Strong shadows falling across the snowdrops cause their colour to vary from white to blue.

24

Achieving perspective

The illusion of depth can be achieved in various ways, which are described below. When combined, they can create a stunningly realistic effect.

With use of colour

Be aware that colours change within a woodland as your eye moves from the foreground to the background; tree foliage will appear brighter and with more contrast in the foreground, and more muted and with a blue-grey hue in the distance. To achieve depth, put together different shades of the same colour rather than a single block of colour; I use a broad tonal range, from very dark to light, for the best effect.

With scale of stitches

Simply explained, the smaller the stitch used the further away an element appears. For the most distant leaves, therefore, set the sewing machine on straight stitch and move the hoop slowly to create a small stitch. The direction in which this stitch is worked is not important, because the detail is so small, so an overall texture created with a small, spiralling straight stitch is very effective.

In the middle distance use a narrow width of zigzag stitch; this is where a more obvious direction can be observed, as the leaves follow the diagonal sweep of a branch. Remember that moving the hoop slowly keeps the stitches small and close together. A variation in texture can be achieved by holding the hoop still occasionally and letting stitches build up upon each other.

In the foreground, leaves should be a larger zigzag stitch and the hoop rotated to make them lie in the right direction. When individual leaves are more apparent, this is an opportunity to 'draw' some shapes by varying the width of zigzag stitch, and to add different colours and tones.

With order of work

One of the most difficult aspects of embroidering woodlands with dense foliage is the order in which you stitch the various elements. It may seem logical to stitch all the trees and then all the bluebells, for example, but this is not always the most successful approach. Try to imagine the scene as a three-dimensional image, and work from the back of the picture to the foreground in layers. You will need to switch methodically from one element to another as you proceed towards the foreground detail, eventually working the foreground branches, tree trunks and woodland flowers so that they overlap each other and push the distant ones even further back.

With the repetition of elements

The repetition of certain elements throughout a design will aid the sense of perspective. These can include shadows, branches, tree trunks or even a colour. As the feature diminishes in size into the distance, the sense of depth is emphasised.

Over the Fence

18 x 13cm (7 x 5in)

The fence posts and trees diminish in size towards the back of the picture, creating depth.

Tree trunks

Tree trunks are usually the strongest feature of a woodland scene. To recreate the huge variety of textures, colours and shapes, there are numerous different machine embroidery techniques that you can use – which you choose depends on how much detail you can observe, and the colour and texture of the bark. To give them a rounded appearance, use the darkest tones down the side of the trunk that is in shadow, and gradually introduce lighter tones as you move round to the side that is facing the sun.

Perspective

To help achieve a sense of perspective, use smaller stitches, a less textured finish and more muted colours as trees diminish in size into the distance. The techniques on these two pages are suitable for various tree types.

This textured foreground tree bark has been created using a series of vertical rows of zigzag stitch, in which the stitch width has been increased and decreased several times along the length of the trunk. A dark bobbin thread, pulled to the surface by increasing the top tension, has been used throughout, and the colour of the top thread has been varied to obtain the gradual change from light to dark.

Autumn in Candy Woods
7.5 x 13cm (3 x 5in)

The main tree trunk was created using vertical, parallel lines of straight stitch, and the background trees were worked in narrow columns of zigzag stitch.

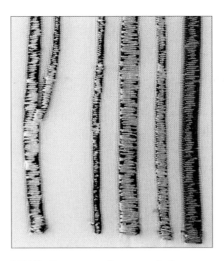

These distant trunks are worked as vertical columns of zigzag stitch, sometimes with a line of straight stitch underneath. The bobbin thread is pulled to the surface by a tight top tension and a darker thread is used in the bobbin than on the top of the machine.

Middle-distance trunks are worked as vertical columns of medium-width zigzag stitch with the bobbin thread pulled to the surface by a tight top tension. Notice the different effects that can be achieved by using different thread colour combinations.

These smooth foreground tree trunks consist of parallel rows of straight stitch worked vertically, in progressively lighter shades as you move across from left to right.

Foreground moss-covered tree trunk

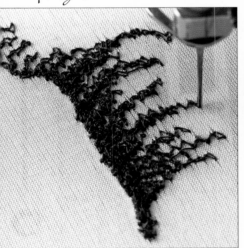

1. Begin by working the dark side of the trunk using a dark brown thread in the bobbin and on the top of the machine. Use parallel lines of straight stitching and follow the curve of the trunk. Make small, jagged, up and down movements of the hoop as you work to create wavy lines of stitching.

2. Work the mossy areas using a dark green thread on the top of the machine and yellow in the bobbin. Use straight stitch and move hoop as before, tightening the top tension to pull the bobbin thread up and create a three-dimensional, textured effect.

3. For the lightest areas, place a lighter yellow in the bobbin and continue working the same stitch to complete the trunk. Remember to curve the lines of stitching around the trunk.

To create a smooth-textured, mossy bark, place the moss-coloured thread in the bobbin and pull it up with a tight top thread. Use parallel lines of straight stitching and vary the shade of the top thread to create areas of light and dark.

This silver textured bark uses a similar technique to that shown on page 26, but with straight stitching worked between the sections of zigzag stitching to add more texture and fill in the gaps.

Foreground lichen-covered tree trunk

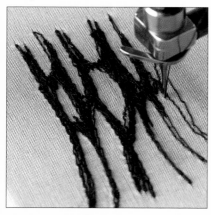

1. First sew the bare bark. Use rows of straight stitching and follow the pattern of the bark, using your source photograph for reference.

2. Replace the bobbin thread with a blue-green, tighten the top tension and loosen the bobbin tension to create loops of bobbin thread on the surface. Work short, jagged straight stitches in between the brown.

3. Continue to fill the spaces in between the bare areas of bark. Use a lighter coloured thread on the top and in the bobbin on one side of the tree to create shading.

Woodland floor

Fallen leaves are often a feature of woodlands and the techniques used to create them vary with distance from the foreground; the scale of the stitches creates a sense of perspective.

Distance

For a woodland floor viewed in the distance, work parallel lines of straight stitch in various colour combinations to form stripes, representing shadows from the trees and foliage.

Distant woodland floor.

Middle distance

1. Work the middle-distance woodland floor as rows of spiralling straight stitch. Begin by working the base with a dark thread on the top and in the bobbin.

2. Gradually introduce different shades and colours until the area is completely filled. Create shaded areas using the darker tones.

This middle-distance area of woodland floor is created by setting the machine on a narrow zigzag stitch and working series of stitches worked on the spot to create individual leaves. Place the rows of stitching in curved, parallel lines, following the contours of the ground.

Foreground

1. Beginning with the darkest colour, work each fallen leaf as a series of zigzag stitches worked on the spot. Leave spaces in between for leaves of other colours.

2. Fill in the gaps using different colours, working through the mid tones to the highlights. Work the stitches in different directions by changing the angle of the hoop.

Foliage

Within densely stitched foliage, the depth of the scene can be expressed by the scale of the stitching. Here are some examples of this.

Distant foliage

Middle-distance and background foliage is worked in curved lines, mimicking the shape of the branches. In each example below, the top tension is tightened to pull up the bobbin thread, and there is a darker shade in the bobbin than on the top.

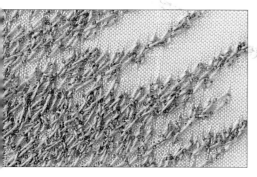

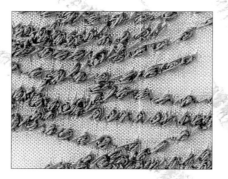

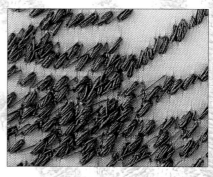

A less textured finish suggests background foliage. Here, straight stitching has been worked in curved lines with small, spiralling movements of the hoop.

For less distant foliage, use curved lines of small zigzag stitches, with some stitches worked on top of each other to suggest individual leaves.

This middle-distance foliage is worked in the same way as that shown on the left, but with a larger stitch.

Foreground foliage

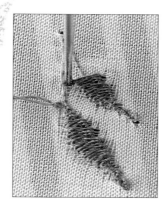

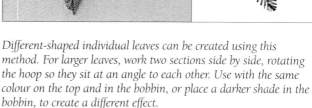

1. Work straight stitch along the stem to the tip of the leaf, then work back again using zigzag stitch, gradually increasing the width of the stitch to form the top part of the leaf.

2. Complete the leaf by gradually reducing the width of the zigzag stitch, then work the next leaf in the same way.

Different-shaped individual leaves can be created using this method. For larger leaves, work two sections side by side, rotating the hoop so they sit at an angle to each other. Use with the same colour on the top and in the bobbin, or place a darker shade in the bobbin, to create a different effect.

Ferns

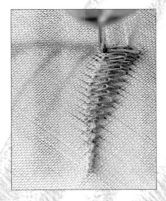 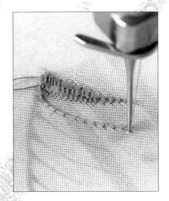 

1. Working from the base of the fern to the tip, stitch along the midrib of the first frond using straight stitch, then work back along it using a widening zigzag.

2. When you reach the stem, change back to straight stitch and work the next frond in the same way. Note: rotate the hoop so that the straight stitching lies vertically under the machine and work the zigzag stitch horizontally across it.

3. Work to the tip of the fern to complete. Observe the shapes of the ferns, and how the fronds gradually diminish in size towards the top and end with a delicate curl at the tip.

Grass

Various techniques can be used for grasses, depending on whether they are in the fore-, middle- or background.

These distant grasses were created using straight stitch worked up and down in vertical and diagonal lines. For more depth, place a few curved blades of grass in front, worked on top of the background grass in a darker shade of green.

For foreground grass, work from the base of each blade of grass with straight stitch, then work back down it with a zigzag, gradually increasing the width of the stitch as you approach the base.

Rosebay willow herb

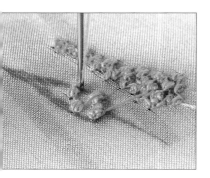

Starting at the base of the flower, create a series of zigzags worked on the spot. Gradually reduce the stitch width as you approach the top of the flower, then increase it again as you work your way back down, filling in the gaps as you go. A darker shade in the bobbin makes the flower look more three-dimensional.

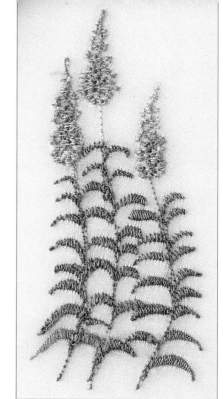

The leaves of the rosebay willow herb are worked in the same way as the foreground foliage on page 30.

Foxgloves and bluebells

1. To create foxgloves, first draw in the stem and a guide line for each trumpet. Use a darker shade in the bobbin than in the top of the machine and tighten the top tension. Work straight stitches from the stem to the end of the first trumpet. Change to a wide zigzag stitch and work back towards the stem, reducing the stitch width as you go to form the trumpet shape.

2. Change back to a straight stitch, sew along the stem and work the next trumpet in the same way.

Completed foxglove flowers; for the stems and leaves, see the rosebay willow herb above.

Bluebells (shown right) are worked in a similar way to foxgloves, but with a constant width of zigzag. This time, however, draw only a single curved line for each flower, then stitch the individual bells by eye. Using a narrow zigzag stitch, work from the top of the stem to the tip of the first bell and back again to the stem, then continue down the stem making a total of five or six bells on each flower.

Rhododendrons

Begin by drawing in the outline of each flower. With a darker shade in the bobbin and a tight top tension to pull the bobbin thread to the surface, work each flower as a series of zigzag stitches radiating out from the base. Reduce the size of the background flowers to create perspective.

Vary the colour and size of the flowers to give depth and added interest to your embroidery. Notice how the angle of the flowers is also important for achieving a realistic effect.

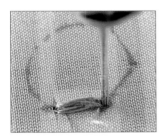   

1. Starting at the base on the left of the flower, use a wide zigzag stitch and sew on the spot to create the first petal.

2. With the needle at the base of the flower, work the next petal in the same way, rotating the hoop a little so that the petals begin to fan out from the base.

3. Complete the first row of petals.

4. Work the remaining rows in the same way, dovetailing each row with the preceding one.

Daffodils

Growing in groups or drifts in a woodland setting, creating daffodils is more about swathes of colour rather than individual flowers (see page 7).

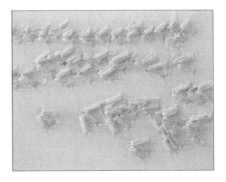

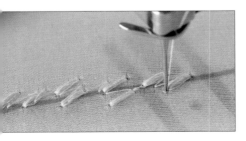 

1. For a cluster of flowers, sew all the petals that lie at the same angle first. Use a wide zigzag stitch and sew on the spot for each petal.

2. Rotate the hoop slightly to alter the angle of the stitching, and add a second petal to each flowerhead.

Completed daffodil heads. If trumpets are required, work these as narrower zigzag stitches laid horizontally and worked in a different shade of yellow.

Creating the background

I begin all my embroideries by transferring my design on to silk with an air/water-soluble pen, marking out the key elements and main areas of the composition with resist to control the flow of the paint. I then paint the background with silk paints. Simple washes are used to fill large areas with colour, then the details are painted on. Preparing the background in this way makes the embroidery stage easier and more logical, allowing you to focus on the sewing without having to worry about the sizes and the layout of the various elements. The coloured background also blends with the stitching more easily than bare white silk, which avoids the possibility of overworking the piece.

Here are two examples of source photographs and the painted backgrounds they inspired. When I have finished painting and the paint has dried, I use a hot iron to fix the image, then wash the silk in hot, soapy water to remove the resist. The white lines that remain can be seen clearly in these two paintings.

In the photograph on the left I identified three main bands of colour in the background which I separated with two lines of resist – the sky, overlaid with foliage; a bank; and the woodland floor. I then drew on the trunk and main branches of the tree.

The photograph above was also divided into horizontal bands, which I painted accordingly, and this time there are two trees, one more shaded and therefore painted darker than the other one. This leads the eye towards the bright patch between them, in the centre of the composition.

Transferring the design

There are several ways of transferring your design to the silk; which one you use depends on your confidence and skill level. If you have good drawing skills, the design can be drawn freehand directly on to the stretched silk, mapping out the key elements and main areas of the composition.

If you prefer, you can transfer the design by placing the source photograph behind the silk when it is stretched on the frame and then tracing over the top of it, again picking out the key elements and main areas. A light box is invaluable if you favour this way of working. This is the method described below. If not enough detail is visible through the silk, then use a tracing of the picture instead, made with tracing paper or acetate and a permanent marker, as this will show through the silk more clearly.

The source photograph for the design.

1. First, pin the silk on the silk frame. Make sure the fabric is straight, then place the first pin in the centre of one edge of the frame, securing it firmly. Continue placing pins along that edge, working from the central pin outwards. Space the pins approximately 8cm (3½in) apart. Work the opposite edge in the same way, ensuring all the time that the fabric is pulled firmly across the frame. Finally, pin the remaining two sides. If you can see strong pull lines between two sides, release the fabric from those edges and re-pin them with a slightly lighter touch.

2. Place your chosen photograph under the silk, lifted up on a raised surface. It should touch the underside of the silk, so that the image shows through clearly on the top. Begin by drawing the border around the image using a metal ruler and an air/water-soluble pen.

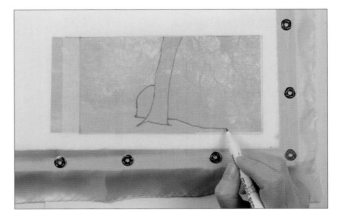

3. Place the main elements, in this case the tree trunk and the large shrub, by tracing around their outlines with the air/water-soluble pen.

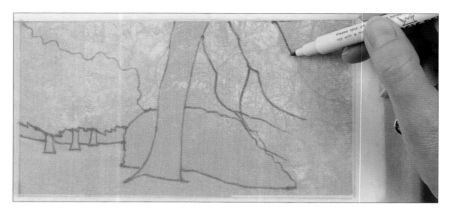

4. Next, draw in the three tree trunks on the left and the ground level behind them, outline the area of solid yellow foliage above, and mark in the positions of the main branches hanging down on the right. The area of yellow foliage on the left is larger than the section I have drawn. I will embroider leaves higher up where white silk will show through between my stitches

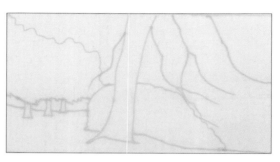

Tip

Leave out any details you do not wish to include.

5. Remove the photograph from behind the silk and check that all the main elements are in place, and that you are happy with your composition.

Painting the design

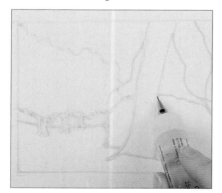

1. Go over every purple line, including the border, with resist using a fine-nibbed applicator. Allow it to dry thoroughly. This will prevent the paint from spreading into adjacent areas.

2. Decide which area you wish to paint first, in this case the woodland floor. Using the photograph for reference, mix a suitable colour in the palette and test it on the silk before applying it to your background (remember that it will dry paler).

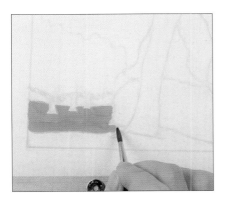

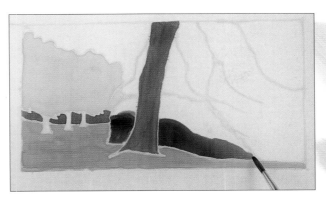

3. When you are happy with the colour (it does not have to be an exact match as you will be stitching over it), apply it as a flat wash to the background. Allow the paint to spread naturally up to the line of resist to fill the area you are painting completely.

4. Paint in the remaining large areas of colour – I have used an undiluted dark brown mix for the main trunk and the area behind the trees in the background, a dilute yellow-brown for the golden foliage on the left, and a strong green for the lower part of the shrub.

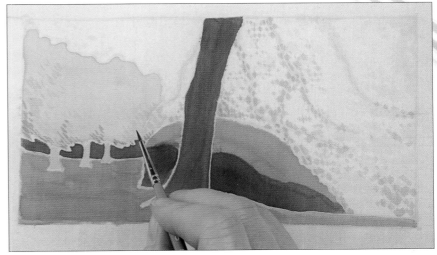

5. Dilute the green mix for the top part of the shrub, and use the same colour to 'dot in' the green leaves behind the main branches on the right. Place them either side of the branches to help retain a guide line, and to give depth to the finished embroidery.

6. Dot in the yellow leaves on the right-hand side of the picture in the same way, and finish by adding dots of yellow and green to the golden foliage on the left, giving it a more three-dimensional feel.

To fix the image

The background now needs to be fixed with a hot iron and washed in hot, soapy water to remove the resist. Dry and iron the silk once more, and it is then ready to be embroidered.

Freehand painting

A background wash in silk paint serves well as the base for this embroidered winter tree. The source photograph was taken in January as the sun was coming up and the colours were changing by the minute. Experiment with sunrises and sunsets in pinks, purples and reds for a dramatic backdrop to a dark grey copse of trees.

By applying the silk paint to the silk without drawing out the design using resist, the colours can flow and blend into each other freely, creating soft edges to each area of colour. It is best to have all the colours you intend to use mixed ready in the palette before you start, so that you can work quickly.

A silhouette of bare branches set against a colourful, early morning sky. This will be worked as a network of lace in dark grey thread across a hole cut in fabric stretched in a hoop.

1. Begin by drawing the border for the picture on silk, pinned on to a silk frame, using air/water-soluble pen. Then make all the colour mixes you think you will need, using the photograph for guidance. Test the colours by placing dots of paint on the silk and allowing it to dry.

Tip

Add more water to a mix for a paler colour; use undiluted paint, straight from the bottle, for a more intense colour.

Tip

When freehand painting, always work with the source photograph alongside and refer to it constantly.

2. Begin the painting by laying down the bands of background colour, starting with the palest. In this case, begin with the band of pale orange across the lower part of the picture, then introduce a little yellow on the right. Use smooth, horizontal brushstrokes, and allow the paint to spread and blend naturally on the silk.

Tip

Always clean and dry your brush in clean water when changing from one colour to another. This prevents unwanted colour mixing and prevents the colours from becoming diluted.

Tip

Work quickly, so that the colours blend freely on the silk while still wet.

3. Without allowing the first colour to dry, introduce the next band of colour (pale blue), blending it carefully with the first using the paintbrush.

4. Next put in the top band of colour – the darker blue across the top of the sky – and blend it with a narrower band of pale orange placed above the light blue.

5. Continuing quickly, introduce more of the pale orange into the blue. Blend some stronger orange into the lighter areas.

6. Bring in the purple tones to deepen the clouds in the top part of the sky. Deepen the lower part of the sky by adding more streaks of orange and yellow.

7. Allow the background to dry and start to strengthen the colours, beginning with the deep purple and orange tones in the main cloud. Use small dots of colour so that they blend in easily.

8. Once dry, continue to strengthen the purple until you have achieved the required depth of colour. Heighten the intensity of the lower part of the picture by introducing patches of pale purple and orange using a tiny brush. Fix the paint with a hot iron.

Creating the silhouette

Stretch some muslin or lightweight calico in a 20cm (8in) hoop. Cut a circular hole 10cm (4in) across in the centre and then re-stretch the fabric; the hole will increase in size as the fabric becomes taut in the hoop. With the machine set on straight stitch, pull up the bobbin thread through the fabric and start stitching across the hole. Move the hoop at a steady pace and simply let the top and bobbin threads twist together across the hole.

Tip
Do not zigzag to the top of the tree – the stitching will look too heavy.

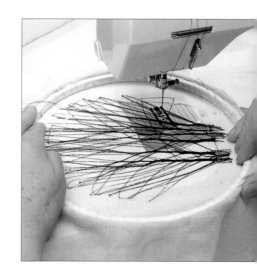

1. Start with a fan-shaped arrangement of straight stitches as the basic structure for the trees, then use zigzag stitch to gather the threads together at the base to form five trunks. Create more branches higher up the trees by criss-crossing the embroidery with straight stitching. Gather some of these together with zigzag stitch. Extend single lines of straight stitching just beyond the top of the tree for a more natural look. Once you have a shape you are happy with, work over it slowly with zigzag stitch to neatly 'bind' the threads together.

2. Cut the lace tree away from the fabric.

3. Stretch the painted background in the bound hoop and pin the tree in place, using the photograph for reference. Stitch it in place using the same thread as you used for the tree.

4. Using straight stitch, work V shapes up and down the top 2cm (¾in) of the branches to hold the silhouette in position. At the same time, create more depth by stitching new, smaller branches on to the background in between the existing ones.

5. Stitch across the base of the trees to secure them.

6. Work series of straight stitches using jagged and spiralling movements of the hoop to create the foliage at the base of the trees.

The completed embroidery.

Springtime

The focal point of this embroidery is the beautiful splash of colour created by the woodland azalea. The embroidery is worked from the back of the picture to the front. Carefully complete each area before moving forwards to the next, overlapping the stitches as you proceed to push the details back and create depth. In the foreground the stitches will be bolder and larger, standing out against the more delicately worked background areas.

I have transferred the design by drawing it freehand directly on to the silk, referring closely to the photograph, but the method you use is entirely up to you (see page 35).

You will need

Resist in a pipette with a fine nib

Full-size copy of the source photograph (or a similar one of your own)

Ruler

Paper, pencil, permanent marker tracing paper and/or acetate for tracing (optional)

Air/water-soluble pen

White, medium-weight silk

Wooden silk frame

Approximately 20 silk pins

Paintbrushes, silk paints and mixing palette

Liquid soap

Iron

Bound 20cm (8in) embroidery hoop

Selection of coloured machine embroidery threads (see the panel down the left-hand side of the page for guidance)

Source photograph

This embroidery is based on the photograph shown on the left without cropping or alteration, as I was happy with the composition. It offers the opportunity for many different techniques, including small, spiralling straight stitches for distant foliage; smooth, closely worked zigzags for tree trunks; large, jagged stitches for the foreground leaves and flowers; and delicately stitched detail for the fern at the base of the tree. This photograph is reproduced at two-thirds of its actual size; to obtain a full-size version, it needs to be scanned or photocopied at 150 per cent.

1. Begin by pinning the silk on the wooden frame, then draw in the border and the main elements in the photograph using an air/water-soluble pen. Begin with the three main tree trunks, then outline the azalea bush and mark in the positions of the main flowers (more flowers can be added when you start to sew). Put in a guide line down the centre of each fern at the base of the foreground tree, and draw in the tree line, slightly lower than in the photograph, to open up the sky a little more. Finally, indicate the positions of the background trees as single lines, and add any details on the ground you can see. Once you are happy with the composition, go over the purple lines with resist and allow it to dry.

Tip

This embroidery is too large to fit in the embroidery hoop, so stretch up the top half first as this is where you need to start.

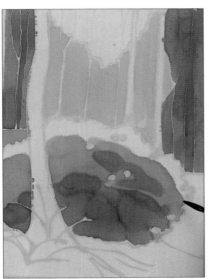

2. Paint the background, beginning with a flat wash of pale yellow-green for the lighter areas of foliage in the background. (Not all of this area will be stitched, so choose the lightest shade visible.) Mix a darker green for the darker areas of foliage and for the lower half of the azalea bush, and a mid green for the upper half. Be careful not to paint over the spaces left for the flowers.

3. Add some more yellow to the pale yellow-green mix for the green areas of ground, and for the spaces left for the flowers, and use a watery mix of black and purple for the tree trunks. Finally, make a mustard-coloured mix for the moss at the base of the tree and the ferns, and add some brown for the area of bare ground beneath the azalea. Allow the paint to dry thoroughly.

4. Iron and wash your work (see page 37), and stretch it in a 20cm (8in) bound embroidery hoop so that the top part of the picture lies within the hoop ready for stitching. Using the background and the photograph for reference, choose a good range of coloured threads (see page 17).

5. Using the darkest green both on the machine and in the bobbin, work the darkest areas of the background. Set the machine on straight stitch, and move the hoop using small, spiralling movements to create texture. Leave gaps for the mid to lighter tones.

6. Leaving the bobbin colour the same, thread a mid-tone green on the machine and use the same stitch to place the mid tones. Overlap the darker areas of stitching slightly to blend them together, and use the lower edge of the stitched foliage to outline the foreground shrub as accurately as possible.

7. Using a very dark brown in the bobbin and a light brown on the top, work the background tree trunks using a narrow zigzag stitch. Start at the base of each trunk and work upwards, tapering the top slightly by making the stitch narrower. Use the same stitch to put in the main branches, working from the trunk towards the end of each branch, tapering down to a straight stitch in some cases.

8. Place the mid-tone green in the bobbin and a lighter, silvery green on the machine, and stitch the lighter areas of foliage as before (steps 5 and 6).

Tip

Remember to refer continually to the source photograph to ensure that the colours and composition remain true to the original. Draw in extra guide lines using the air/water-soluble pen if necessary.

9. Stitch foliage around some of the branches and across the sky, overlapping some of the background tree trunks. Keep these stitches tiny so that they recede into the distance. Retain accurate outlines around the foreground elements (in this case the main tree trunk on the left and the shrub) to maintain their size and shape.

10. For the main tree trunks on the right, use grey thread in the bobbin and white on the machine. Work them from the bottom upwards using a wide zigzag stitch. Change to a white bobbin thread, and use a narrower zigzag to place a white highlight down the right-hand side of each tree. Take it only halfway up the tree in the mid-ground.

11. Using mid green in the bobbin and light green on the machine, stitch the foliage overlaying the top of the right-hand tree. Make the stitches larger than before so that they stand out from the background.

12. Add highlights to this foliage and to the shrubs on the right using the light, silvery green in the bobbin and an even paler green on the top. Use straight stitch and move the hoop using jagged movements to create a series of 'V' shapes, so that it looks different from the distant foliage.

13. Work the top part of the main foreground trunk as three overlapping columns of zigzag stitch, using the same threads as before (step 10). This time, tighten the top tension so that more of the bobbin colour shows through.

14. Place a white highlight down the right-hand side (see step 10).

15. Put the grey back in the bobbin and put a darker grey on the top, and use straight stitch to place the dark markings going across the trunk with small, horizontal stitches.

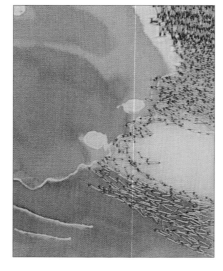

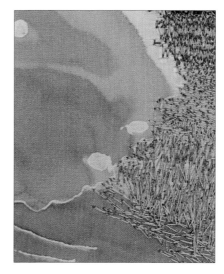

16. Move the fabric in the hoop so that the lower part of the embroidery lies within it. Stitch the small area of grass on the right, just below the trees, using the mid green in the bobbin and the light, silvery green used in step 12 on the top. Use straight stitch and work in horizontal rows, moving the hoop up and down sharply to create small, jagged stitches.

17. Work the areas of bare ground to the right of the azalea using a light, pinky brown on the top and a darker tone in the bobbin. Work in straight stitch back and forth across the work, following the slope of the ground.

18. For the grassy patch near the foreground, use a more yellowy green. Put a dark tone in the bobbin and a mid tone on the top of the machine, and repeat the jagged straight stitches you used in step 16, making them slightly longer. Put the mid tone in the bobbin and a lighter tone on the top, and add a few highlights using the same stitch.

Tip

Your original design is for guidance only; adapt it, if necessary, as your work progresses, and draw in extra detail if required.

19. Using the air/water-soluble pen, draw in the outlines of the main light-coloured leaves on the azalea for guidance.

20. Stitch the darkest areas between the leaves you have drawn on, avoiding the spaces left for the flowers and the lines drawn for the ferns. Use dark green in the bobbin and in the top of the machine and sew around the leaf shapes using small, jagged straight stitches.

21. Leave dark green in the bobbin and place mid green on the top. Work the shapes at the top of the shrub using the same stitch as before, and the mid-tone leaves lower down. For each leaf, use three or four straight stitches worked back and forth on the same spot. To make larger stitches, run the machine slowly and move your hands more quickly.

22. Move the mid green to the bobbin and place a paler green on top, and work the lighter leaves higher up on the azalea. Complete the shrub by stitching the lightest-coloured leaves at the top using the paler green in the bobbin and a pale silvery green on the top. Remember to leave spaces for the flowers.

23. For the darkest flowers, use the darkest shade of pink in the bobbin and a mid-tone pink on top of the machine. Work each flower using spiky straight stitches. Add more flowers, if you wish, for more colour. Move the mid tone to the bobbin and place a lighter tone on the top for the light pink flowers towards the top of the bush.

24. Complete the main tree trunk using the same method as before (see steps 13 to 15). Take the highlight approximately two-thirds of the way down. Finish by placing a few bands of straight stitching across the trunk using pale lilac thread in the top of the machine and grey in the bobbin.

25. For the area underneath the azalea, place a very dark brown in the bobbin and a dark brown on the top. Work small, spiralling straight stitches in curved rows, following the roots of the tree and the slope of the ground. Use the same colours for the dark areas behind the ferns. Work these in jagged lines of straight stitching to define the fronds.

26. With two shades of pinky brown as before (see step 17), work the lighter areas using the same technique. Overlap the darker areas slightly so that they blend together.

27. Change to a pale mustard yellow on the top of the machine and a deeper version in the bobbin, and work the moss covering the lower part of the main trunk. Use straight stitches worked in compact, wavy lines.

28. For the ferns, place dark green in the bobbin and a fresh blue-green on the top. Lay a foundation of dark leaves for the lighter leaves to stand out against, worked using jagged lines of straight stitching (as in step 25).

29. Move the blue-green to the bobbin and place a light yellow green on top, and place the mid-tone ferns. Work each frond by straight stitching from the base to the end of the frond, then zigzagging back again. Increase the width of the stitch towards the stem (see page 31).

30. Complete the ferns by replacing the bobbin thread with off-white and stitching the foreground leaves. Use the same stitches as before, and refer closely to the photograph to ensure the correct positioning and angle of the leaves.

The completed embroidery.

Details of the completed embroidery.

50

Lake Vyrnwy Woodland
18 x 13cm (7 x 5in)

*The bright yellow-green foliage, typical of spring, and glimpses of a
distant azalea, make this embroidery a favourite for this time of year.*

Rhododendrons at Highfield
18 x 13cm (7 x 5in)

*Always a riot of colour in the springtime,
this corner of my garden has been an
inspiration for many of my embroideries.*

Sunlit Path

The strong tonal contrast drew my eye to this scene; the bright sunlight creates wonderful dark shadows, and flashes of dramatic light cutting through the trees form stripes across the woodland path. The dark brown tree trunks form strong verticals, and contrast with the lush greens and yellows of the summer foliage.

Working from the background to the foreground section by section, allow areas to overlap a little to create the illusion of depth. Remember that depth can also be achieved by altering the scale of the stitching (smaller stitches in the distance and larger, more textured stitching at the front of the picture).

You will need

Resist in a pipette with a fine nib

Full-size copy of the source photograph (or a similar one of your own)

Ruler

Paper, pencil, permanent marker tracing paper and/or acetate for tracing (optional)

Air/water-soluble pen

White, medium-weight silk

Wooden silk frame

Approximately 20 silk pins

Paintbrushes, silk paints and mixing palette

Liquid soap

Iron

Bound 20cm (8in) embroidery hoop

Selection of coloured machine embroidery threads (see the panel down the left-hand side of the page for guidance)

Source photograph

Cropping this photograph emphasises the tall tree on the left-hand side. The final size is 10 x 18cm (4 x 7in). To obtain a full-size version, it needs to be scanned or photocopied at 150 per cent.

1. Pin the silk on the silk frame, then draw in the border and the main elements in the photograph using an air/water-soluble pen – the foreground tree and its main branches, the ground level, the main areas of foliage and the round patch of light at the bottom on the right of the picture. Compare your drawing with the photograph and, once you are happy with the composition, go over the purple lines with resist and allow it to dry.

Tip

Here I have transferred the design by drawing it freehand directly on to the silk, referring closely to the photograph, but the method you use is entirely up to you (see page 35). If you are not happy with your drawing, add any extra details you feel are needed, or leave out some of the detail to simplify the picture.

2. Mix a very pale yellow to match the lightest background colour you can see. Apply the colour to the background, behind the trees and over the round light patch, to give the whole picture a warm glow. Create a yellow-green mix and 'dot

3. Mix a darker yellow-green and put in the darker areas within the foliage. This will help you observe where the different areas of colour are in the picture.

4. Use a strong mix of black and brown for the tree trunks and branches, and a dilute version of the same mix for the ground. When the paint has dried completely, fix it in the normal way (see page 37).

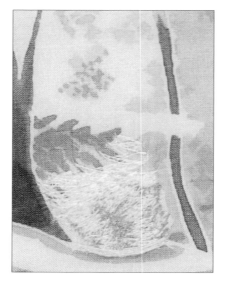

6. Starting with the round patch of sunlight bottom right, place white in the bobbin and a pale yellow-green on the top. Work the darkest areas in the centre and on either side using diagonal rows of tiny straight stitches. For the lighter areas, pull the bobbin thread up by tightening the tension on the top of the machine. Add highlights by placing white on the top of the machine and sewing in between the existing stitching.

5. Place your work in a bound 20cm (8in) hoop and select your thread colours, using the photograph and the painted background as reference.

Tip

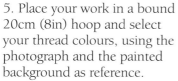

You will need a wide range of yellow-greens for the more distant areas, a smaller range of blue-greens for the foreground foliage, and a selection of dark and warm browns for the tree trunks and woodland floor (see page 52).

7. Using white in the bobbin and pale yellow on the top of the machine, put in the backlighting. Stitching in between the foliage, use straight stitches worked with small spiralling movements in diagonal and horizontal curves.

8. For the mid-tone areas of background foliage, put a bright yellow-green on the machine and a paler version in the bobbin. Fill the mid-tone areas using straight stitch and tiny spiralling movements of the hoop, working back and forth across the embroidery. Avoid stitching over the tree trunks.

9. Put a very dark brown thread on the top and in the bobbin, and stitch parallel rows of straight stitch up and down the background tree trunks. Use the same colours for the shadows behind the trees and the dark shadow lying across the path below the round patch of sunlight.

10. For the dark foliage in the distance, either side of the path, put a very dark green on the top of the machine and in the bobbin. For a delicate look, work numerous tiny straight stitches, as in step 8, leaving sufficient space within the stitched areas for the background to show through. Allow these stitches to overlap the round patch of sunlight.

11. Use the same yellow-greens as those used in step 8 – the paler version on the top and the brighter one in the bobbin. Continue placing the mid tones within the lower areas of background foliage, this time stitching across the tree trunks to bring the foliage forward, and using small spiralling stitches to create texture. Stitch the strip of bright green grass along the distant edge of the bank in the same way.

Tip

Woodland scenes may require the lighter tones to be stitched first, depending on the layering of the elements from front to back. In this case the sunlit areas of foliage in the background need to be worked before the darker foreground areas.

12. Continuing within the same area, including the grassy bank, place the pale yellow-green in the bobbin and pale yellow on the top of the machine, and put in the lighter tones.

13. Leave the same colour in the bobbin and place the bright yellow-green on the top, and work the darker areas higher up on the background foliage.

Tip

Follow the line and shape of the branches when stitching the foliage, referring constantly to the photograph, to produce a realistic effect. Draw in as many guide lines as you need with the air/water-soluble pen.

14. With dark brown in the bobbin and a mid-tone brown on the top, begin to stitch the woodland floor – the lighter area lying just beyond the shaft of light, and the mid-tone areas in the foreground. Towards the front of the picture, use larger stitches worked in spiralling movements to create more texture and depth (see page 29).

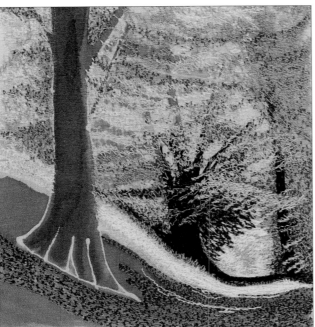

15. Place white thread in the bobbin and on the top of the machine and work the brightest sunlit areas of the woodland floor. Use horizontal rows of straight stitch where the main shaft of light crosses the path, jagged straight stitches on the bank, and tiny, spiralling stitches for the smaller patch of light towards the foreground.

16. Replace the top thread with a bright yellow-green and put in the strip of grass along the edge of the sunlit area toward the front of the picture. Use small, jagged stitches to mimic the blades of grass.

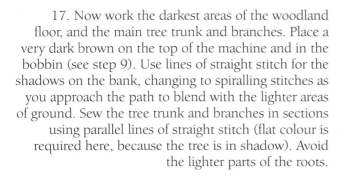

17. Now work the darkest areas of the woodland floor, and the main tree trunk and branches. Place a very dark brown on the top of the machine and in the bobbin (see step 9). Use lines of straight stitch for the shadows on the bank, changing to spiralling stitches as you approach the path to blend with the lighter areas of ground. Sew the tree trunk and branches in sections using parallel lines of straight stitch (flat colour is required here, because the tree is in shadow). Avoid the lighter parts of the roots.

18. Replace the top colour with a mid brown, and place the lighter highlights down the right-hand side of the trunk and the vertical branches, and on the roots. Use the same colours to blend together the lighter and darker parts of the ground you have already stitched.

19. Change to a very dark green on the top and yellow in the bobbin, and stitch the dark areas of foreground foliage. The inclusion of yellow helps break up the lines of stitching, and this, coupled with the use of tiny stitches and small, spiralling movements of the hoop, produces a delicate, lacy effect.

20. Move the very dark green to the bobbin and place a mid green on the top. Using the same technique, stitch the lighter areas of foreground foliage, blending them with the darker tones that went in the first.

21. Using yellow in the bobbin and lime green on the top of the machine, strengthen the sunlit parts of the foliage. Use the same technique as in steps 19 and 20 to fill small, sunlit patches within the foliage.

Tip

As you get to the end of your embroidery, assess and compare the balance and quantity of colours with the source photograph. To aid this process, place both the embroidery and the photograph upside down and view them from a short distance.

The completed embroidery.

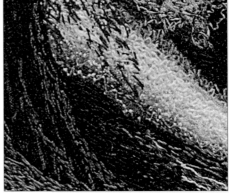

Details of the finished embroidery.

Spring Walk
13 x 18cm (5 x 7in)

This picture works, even though I have broken a design rule and placed the trees in the centre of the composition. The horizontal and diagonal lines are also an important aspect of the design of this embroidery.

Mossy Tree
13 x 18cm (5 x 7in)

A smooth trunk on the foreground tree was worked with parallel lines of straight stitch. The lichen was added last using a light grey bobbin thread pulled to the surface to provide a little texture.

Candy Woods

18 x 13cm (7 x 5in)

This is one of my favourite places at the height of summer, when the trees are heavy with lush, green foliage. I revisited this scene with my camera later in the year after a sudden fall of snow; the embroidery I created from it is shown on page 15.

The Lower Falls

18 x 13cm (7 x 5in)

The foreground water is painted, contrasting well with the texture of the moss-covered rocks, foliage and waterfall.

Fallen Leaves

A strong tree dominates this scene, with its foliage trailing down to the ground on the right. The path, sweeping away to the left, leads the eye into the distance past an avenue of beech trees. Rich autumnal colours and textures made this composition irresistible.

To transfer the design and paint the background, follow the steps on pages 35 to 37.

the steps on pages 35 to 37.

You will need

Resist in a pipette with a fine nib

Full-size copy of the source photograph (or a similar one of your own)

Ruler

Paper, pencil, permanent marker tracing paper and/or acetate for tracing (optional)

Air/water-soluble pen

White, medium-weight silk

Wooden silk frame

Approximately 20 silk pins

Paintbrushes, silk paints and mixing palette

Liquid soap

Iron

Bound 20cm (8in) embroidery hoop

Selection of coloured machine embroidery threads (see the panel down the left-hand side of the page for guidance)

Source photograph

I took sections from two photographs of the same scene to compose this embroidery, placing the tree in the centre of the picture and retaining the pathway on the left. The composite photograph shown here is reproduced at two-thirds of its actual size; to obtain a full-size version, it needs to be scanned or photocopied at 150 per cent.

Tip

You nearly always stitch the darkest tones first and work towards the lightest, so it is a good idea to load a number of bobbins with the darkest tone of each colour before you begin. Make sure you select a broad tonal range of each colour.

1. Once you have washed and ironed your work to fix the image (see page 37), stretch it in a 20cm (8in) embroidery hoop so that the left-hand side of the design falls within the hoop, as this is the side you will embroider first. Select a good range of threads, matching them to the photograph and to the painted background.

2. Start with the darkest areas first, starting with those beneath the yellow background foliage. Place a very dark green in the bobbin and dark green on the top, and fill the area with tiny, spiralling straight stitches. Take the stitching up into the lower parts of the foliage using a more open stitch.

3. Move to the darkest areas of the woodland floor. Place dark brown in the bobbin and a soft mid brown on the top, and sew horizontal, parallel rows of small straight stitches, following the curve of the ground. Work from the background forwards, changing to a longer stitch as you approach the foreground worked in a tight spiralling movement to create texture. Also work the shadows beneath the three trees in the background.

4. Put the soft mid brown in the bobbin and a light, golden brown on the top of the machine, and use the same stitch to fill in the lighter areas of ground.

5. Complete the ground by working your way through three or four further colour combinations, finishing with the highlights. Each time, move the top colour to the bobbin and place a lighter shade on the top.

6. For the background tree trunks, work parallel rows of straight stitches using dark brown in the bobbin and on the top. Replace the top colour with a green-brown and place a line of stitching down the centre of each trunk. Finally, change to a paler brown on the top and stitch the highlight down the right-hand side.

7. Place a deep, golden yellow on the top of the machine and a mid blue-green in the bobbin, and work the darker shades within the yellow background foliage. Work lines of straight stitching, some spiralled, on a curve from left to right.

8. Place three or four more layers of stitching, working progressively lighter areas by moving the top colour to the bobbin and placing a lighter shade on the top. Finish with a very pale yellow on the top for the highlights. Carefully overlap the tree trunks and the dark green stitching behind them.

Tip

If the palest tone you have selected does not stand out as strongly as you would like, replace the bobbin thread with white.

9. Moving to the large shrub, place very dark green on the top and in the bobbin, and work the darkest areas at the base and in the middle using spiralling straight stitches.

10. Keep the very dark green in the bobbin and place a bright mid green on the top, and work the mid-tone areas in the same way. For the lightest parts of the shrub, mainly at the top, move the top colour to the bobbin and replace it with a light green.

11. Having completed the right-hand side of the embroidery, move the hoop to the right and complete the pale green foliage on the right of the picture using the same threads. For the distant foliage behind the branches of the main tree, use light green on the top and white in the bobbin, and work tiny, spiralling straight stitches to give the impression of distance. Do not work the stitches too densely – allow the sky to show through.

12. Complete the small area of ground on the right (see steps 3 to 5). For the main tree, place a very dark brown on the top and in the bobbin. Sew several parallel rows of stitching down the left-hand side of the trunk, working top to bottom. Replace the top colour with dark brown and fill the middle portion of the trunk using the same stitch. Also stitch in the main branches, using straight stitch for the finer branches and zigzag stitch for the broader ones. Adjust the width of the zigzag depending on the width of the branch, and place the finest branches first.

13. Move the dark brown to the bobbin and place a lighter brown on the top, and stitch the mid-tone areas towards the right-hand side of the tree trunk. For the lightest areas, place the top colour in the bobbin and a lighter shade still on the top. Use the same threads to sew the wispiest branches, using straight stitch. Change the top colour to mid green and work the lichen-covered, lower part of the tree trunk. Work in rows, following the curve of the roots. The brown thread in the bobbin helps blend the colour with the rest of the trunk.

14. Place the foreground leaves on the main tree, starting with the darkest ones. For these, use dark yellow on the top and in the bobbin, and set the machine to zigzag stitch. Hold the hoop still while you work each leaf, allowing the zigzag stitch to build up into the form of a leaf. Work different-sized leaves, and vary the direction in which they lie. Refer to the photograph as you work.

15. Put a strong mid yellow on the top, retaining the same colour in the bobbin, and stitch the lighter leaves in the same way. Finally, move the strong mid yellow to the bobbin and place a paler yellow on the top for the palest leaves, most of which are at the top of the tree. Use the widest zigzag setting to make the large foreground leaves.

The completed embroidery.

Details of the finished embroidery.

An Autumn Journey
10 x 18cm (4 x 7in)

The colour of the tree trunks and foliage becomes paler in the distance.

The Richness of Autumn
18 x 13cm (7 x 5in)

With only a few leaves left to fall, all the autumn shades are on the woodland floor in this embroidery.

Winter Snow

The blue sky and shadows, dark grey trees and snow-covered hawthorn trees make this a striking winter composition. A limited palette, and therefore the smallest number of threads, was selected for this project, and there is the opportunity to practise your freehand painting skills (see pages 38–40).

You will need

Resist in a pipette with a fine nib

Full-size copy of the source photograph (or a similar one of your own)

Ruler

Paper, pencil, permanent marker tracing paper and/or acetate for tracing (optional)

Air/water-soluble pen

White, medium-weight silk

Wooden silk frame

Approximately 20 silk pins

Paintbrushes, silk paints and mixing palette

Liquid soap

Iron

Bound 20cm (8in) embroidery hoop

Selection of coloured machine embroidery threads (see the panel down the left-hand side of the page for guidance)

Source photograph
There is an even proportion of painted and stitched areas in this picture, both of equal importance. This photograph is reproduced full-size.

1. Pin the silk on the silk frame, and draw in the main elements using an air/water-soluble pen. Begin by breaking the composition down into three areas of colour, then adding just the bases of the shrubs in the foreground. Go over the lines with resist and allow it to dry completely.

2. Paint the sky by laying progressively darker bands of colour from the horizon upwards, starting with clear water, and allowing the colours to blend naturally on the silk. Place lines of resist where bands of sunlight are shining through the trees in the distance. This will leave white lines on the silk once the resist is removed.

3. Paint the central blue area, making the mix more dilute as you approach the foreground, and the light green area at the front of the picture.

4. Change to a very small brush, and add patches of blue-grey to the area lying behind the trees on the distant slope. Build up the colour gradually using tiny dots of paint rather than sweeping movements of the brush. Finally, draw in the background tree trunks, and the two trees and the fence in the mid-ground (these will not be stitched and will therefore remain part of the background).

5. Once you have ironed and then washed your painting to fix the image, stretch it in a 20cm (8in) hoop and select your threads, referring to both the photograph and the painted background.

6. Stitch the most distant trees with a very pale blue in the bobbin and very dark grey on the top (the pale bobbin thread will help break up the lines of stitching and produce a delicate, lacy effect). Draw in the branches first using tiny straight stitches, starting at the top and working downwards into the trunks.

7. Replace the bobbin thread with dark blue and, using straight stitch, work the hedge running along the horizon from the right, and the trees growing further down the hillside.

8. Place mid blue in the bobbin (retaining the very dark grey on the top) and soften the trunks into the background by placing horizontal rows of straight stitch between them to represent the shadows. Add more small trees to the left and within the main woodland area. Finally, use straight stitch for the boundary at the base of the slope.